The Healing POWER of Faith

W0006894

TWENTY-THIRD PUBLICATIONS
185 WILLOW STREET • PO BOX 180 • MYSTIC, CT 06355
TEL: 1-800-321-0411 • FAX: 1-800-572-0788
E-MAIL: ttpubs@aol.com • www.twentythirdpublications.com
Bayard

NOVALIS

Twenty-Third Publications
A Division of Bayard
185 Willow Street
P.O. Box 180
Mystic, CT 06355
(860) 536-2611 or (800) 321-0411
www.twentythirdpublications.com
ISBN:1-58595-322-9

Published in Canada by
Novalis
49 Front Street East, 2nd Floor
Toronto, Ontario, Canada
M5E 1B3
Phone: 1-800-387-7164 or (416) 363-3303
Fax: 1-800-204-4140 or (416) 363-9409
Email: cservice@novalis-inc.com
ISBN: 2-89507-466-6

Library of Congress Catalog Card Number: 2003113498
Canadian Catalog Number: C2004-900970-2
Printed in the U.S.A.

Contents

"Why, God, why?" we often ask in times of trouble. Such a question requires not only an intellectual answer, but an existential one that deals with the deepest level of our destiny.

This question may be asked by a skeptic who cannot understand why things are the way they are, or by a believer who is starting a prayer as the psalmist did, "Why, O Lord, do you stand far off? Why do you hide yourself in times of trouble?" (Ps 10:1).

In either case, this question says that we are in trouble. But it also reveals that nonbelievers as well as saints have their own histories. People do not become nonbelievers or saints overnight. They are formed, not born, to be the way they are.

Who among us, at one time or another, has not felt disappointed, frustrated, and even betrayed? Who among us can declare with certainty that he or she is safe from accidents, wars, or terrorism? We are always facing the possibility of trouble. Often it seems as if no one—even in heaven—cares. So some people declare that God, not evil, is dead.

Faith in God?! It is difficult to be a person of faith in today's world. We are exhausted by a deluge of words, opinions, doctrines, and slogans—an information overload. We are frustrated by the conflicting propaganda launched by the media and self-interest groups. We are immersed in a noisy world full of distractions and intoxicated by success and power. We are captivated by a religion that is beautifully packaged and presented by people we are supposed to trust and admire, but who sometimes disappoint us by their actions and decisions. We seem to have lost the capacity for deep and simple trust.

Nevertheless, trust and true faith are the answer to our malaise.

If we think about faith, we realize that, besides its theological roots, it is the most practical and down-to-earth aspect of our lives. Without faith, our lives would be almost impossible to sustain. In fact, we rely on faith all the time.

We have faith in the electricity we use, the food we eat, the water we drink, the car we drive, and the bridge we cross. We don't spend time analyzing the adequacy of all these things. We choose our friends, we deposit our money in the bank, we mail a letter, we go to the doctor, we take the prescribed medicine because we have faith, and we don't necessarily think about any of these things. Life becomes unlivable if we don't have faith. We wouldn't be sure of ourselves. We wouldn't be able to dream, change, dare, live, love, even survive.

The same is true at the spiritual level. Faith is to our spiritual life as breathing is to our physical life. We can't have life if we don't breathe; we can't have spiritual life if we don't have faith.

To be able to say, "I believe" (Jn 9:38) and "I keep the Lord always before me" (Ps 16:8) makes all the difference in the world. Faith in God changes our entire perspective regarding our lives and the world, and creates

> Faith in God changes our entire perspective about our lives and about the world.

a whole new reality. Whatever seemed essential from a worldly point of view may become unnecessary and even despicable; whatever was neglected may become the object of ardent pursuit. Faith gives us a new outlook from which we see different realities.

Faith, however, cannot really be separated from hope and love. As St. Paul wrote (1 Cor 13:13), these three work together to lead us to God and to the fulfillment of the divine purpose of our lives. Faith, hope, and love are true and alive when they form a synthesis. The three, together and in intimate connection, are essential for living an abundant life.

Brother Laurence, in *The Practice of the Presence of God,* says, "All things are possible to him who believes; still more to him who hopes; still more to him who loves; and most of all to him who practices all three." While people of every age, religion, and culture have always believed, hoped, and loved, Christians believe, hope, and love because of the one who revealed himself as "the way, and the truth, and the life" (Jn 14:6).

In this book we will talk about faith; hope and love will be addressed in upcoming books in this series. In the meantime, have faith and read on.

CHAPTER ONE

Why Is It So Hard to Find God?

"The worship of idols not to be named is the beginning and cause and end of every evil."

■ WISDOM 14:27

Since the beginning of time, the relationship between human beings and God has never been clear, transparent, or easy.

We know that we were created in the image of God (Gen 1:26). We also know that throughout history we have crafted God in our own image.

5

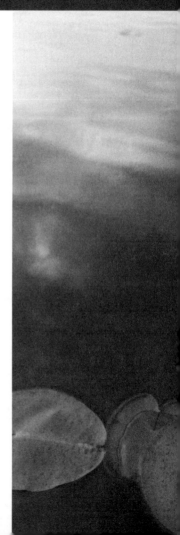

> As a people, we tend to believe in God, but we often act as if God does not exist.

We have created many gods. In fact, our gods are as numerous as our cultures, as different as our ways of thinking and our moods. The *Encyclopedia of Gods* names more than 2,500 deities that humankind has worshiped, gods for almost every aspect and need of human life.

Sometimes, however, we declare the "death of God," as we have done at various times during the last two centuries. Indeed, the philosophies of Ludwig Feuerbach, Karl Marx, Charles Darwin, Friedrich Nietzsche, Sigmund Freud, and others did not leave room for the God we know. For them and their followers, if God was not yet dead, it was the duty of emancipated human beings to kill God.

Today, we are supposedly more sophisticated. As a people, we overwhelmingly tend to believe in God, but we often act as if God does not exist. We go to church, but we ignore Jesus' teachings to be peaceful and just and to love one another. We can give eloquent speeches about how to behave toward others, but too often we don't practice what we preach. We talk the talk, but we don't walk the walk. We pray, but we do what we want to do anyway. This kind of living can perhaps be called "practical atheism."

Since we cannot endure emptiness and desolation, we tend to fill the vacuum by replacing God with idols—modern gods such as money, prestige, power, position, social status, pleasure, possessions, and the like. "The worship of idols not to be named is the beginning and cause and end of every evil" (Wis 14:27). "All the gods of the peoples are idols" (1 Chr 16:26). By acting like this, believers are often responsible for the birth of atheism. The Second Vatican Council describes it with these words:

> Believers can have more than a little to do with the birth of atheism. To the extent that they neglect their own training in the faith, or teach erroneous doctrine, or are deficient in their religious, moral, or social life, they must be said to conceal rather than reveal the authentic face of God and religion (*Gaudium et Spes*, 19).

Unfortunately, many of our institutions have—whether intentionally or not—done more to undermine the truth than to defend it. Yet in spite of all this, God never ceases to speak to us. Why can't we grasp the subtle tones of the divine language?

How Does God Speak?

How do we know God? How can we be sure that our paths to God are the right ones? How do we know the One who said: "I am the Lord your God....You shall have no other gods before me....You shall not make for yourself an idol" (Ex 20:2–4)?

God deals with us as we are. God came to us in the thunder, the breeze, the burning bush, the Ten Commandments, the voices of the prophets, and especially in the Incarnation and in all that springs from the Incarnation.

God's revelation comes to us through the Bible, nature, church, conscience, and especially Jesus Christ. All of these are God's textbooks where we can learn ample details about God.

In the Bible God spoke verbally and by inspiration. The writers of the Bible affirmed that God gave them their material. What they wrote has withstood the attacks of skeptics, agnostics, and atheists, and has been confirmed by the discoveries of archaeologists and scientists. The apostle Paul said, "All scripture is inspired by God" (2 Tim 3:16). The apostle Peter said: "No prophecy ever came by human will, but men and women moved by the Holy Spirit spoke from God" (2 Pet 1:21).

God is also revealed in nature. "The heavens are telling the glory of God; and the firmament proclaims his handiwork. Day to day pours forth speech, and night to night declares knowledge. There is no speech, nor are there words; their voice is not heard" (Ps 19:1–3). We can only stand in awe when we focus our attention on nature in all its beauty, order, laws, intelligence, immensity, complexity, majesty, and mystery. This is why the psalmist wrote, "Fools say in their hearts, 'There is no God'" (Ps 14:1).

God's revelation comes to us through the Bible, nature, church, conscience, and especially Jesus Christ.

The true God resides in the church, to whom the interpretation of revelation is entrusted. The *Catechism of the Catholic Church* describes the role of the church with these words:

The Church, a communion living in the faith of the apostles which she transmits, is the place where we know the Holy Spirit:

• in the Scriptures he inspired;

• in the Tradition, to which the Church Fathers are always timely witnesses;

• in the Church's Magisterium, which he assists;

• in the sacramental liturgy, through its words and symbols, in which the Holy Spirit puts us into communion with Christ;

• in prayer, wherein he intercedes for us;

• in the charisms and ministries by which the Church is built up;

• in the signs of apostolic and missionary life;

• in the witness of saints through whom he manifests his holiness and continues the work of salvation (No. 688).

In our conscience, which speaks to us from the depth of our being, we can detect the imprint of God. When alive and healthy, conscience is God's voice speaking to our souls. St. Bernard says, "A good conscience is a mine of wealth. And in truth what greater riches can there be, what thing more sweet than a good conscience?" Conscience, light of the soul and heart, is our counselor and teacher. It can tell us when we do good or wrong. This is why it is imperative to keep it strong and well-informed. If we don't, it can lead us where we don't wish to go.

In our basic dissatisfaction with human accomplishments, in our insatiable thirst for love, and in our continuous longing for the Infinite, we can feel the absence and the presence of God. "O Lord..." confesses St. Augustine loudly, "you have made us for yourself and our hearts are restless until they can find peace in you."

In the person of Jesus Christ who is "the way, and the truth, and the life" (Jn 14:6), and in whom God speaks clearly, we can be sure of the ultimate truth. The Bible speaks in many ways about Christ, using a multitude of terms:

"The Word became flesh and lived among us, and we have seen his glory, the glory of a father's only son, full of grace and truth" (Jn 1:14).

"When the fullness of time had come, God sent his Son, born of a woman" (Gal 4:4).

"[God] was revealed in flesh" (1 Tim 3:16).

"In him the whole fullness of deity dwells bodily" (Col 2:9).

"Believe in God, believe also in me" (Jn 14:1).

"No one has ever seen God. It is God the only Son, who is close to the Father's heart, who has made him known" (Jn 1:18).

"God...has spoken to us by a Son...through whom he also created the worlds" (Heb 1:1–2).

Surely, this manifestation of God is by far the most complete and the most tangible revelation God ever gave the world. If we want to know God truly and thoroughly, and if we have any hope for peace, joy, justice, mercy, and love, then we have to take a long look at Jesus Christ, who perfectly embodied the fullness of life—divine life itself. Jesus, who has made the unknown known and the unseen seen, has brought the true solution to our world's confusions, limitations, and frustrations. By knowing and living Christ, we will find abundant medicine for all our ailments and problems.

We must see God in our neighbor, of whom God said, "Truly I tell you, just as you did it to one of the least of these who are members of my family, you did it to me" (Mt 25:40).

The Ultimate Authority

What is our answer to the question "Who is the ultimate authority in our lives?" If we answer, "We are" without referring to God in any way, then in practice we are nonbelievers. We don't have to obey a bishop, a guru, an enlightened person, a saint, or any rule outside our own self-made rule. We just rely on our own knowledge, intuition, and experience. We are our own authority. We decide what we believe, how we behave, and what to practice or not practice. We create an idol that is convenient for us and we adore it.

A subtle aspect of seeing self as the authority is that it affects our ideologies. That is, this authority wrongly persuades us that our particular view of reality—our ideology—is absolute truth.

In general, ideologies refer to a set of ideas, beliefs, and patterns that provide a framework for a philosophy about how people should live. These ideologies eventually enable a certain group to have the maximum control over others with a minimum of conflict. The success of a social ideology consists in the ability of one group or one person to coerce another group or person to act in a certain way, not by using force but rather by convincing them how the world works and should work.

In this sense, it is easy to inspire or to lead astray an entire generation or country if leaders succeed in directing people toward a noble goal or a degrading

> By knowing and living Christ, we will find abundant medicine for all our ailments and problems.

one. This leadership can be carried out through schools, places of worship, media, literature, music, advertising, TV, the Internet, or any other cultural form that affects people. Ideologies alter people's perceptions in a positive way as well as in a negative way.

French philosopher Louis Althusser says, "Ideology has very little to do with 'consciousness'—it is profoundly unconscious." He also believes that ideology creates us as persons: it "hails" us, or calls us into being. Even though Althusser seems to go too far here, he makes a point.

Consider the forms we usually use to communicate: the languages, clichés, concepts, categories, symbols, and ways of thinking. Consider the "us" vs. "them" pattern often used in our discourse. Consider our definitions of what is "normal," "natural," "common sense," "loyal," "traitor." Consider racism, sexism, and hierarchical divisions. Consider the values system we have and the priorities that run our lives. Consider the biased tendency of social/political groups, magazines, newspapers, or radio and TV stations. Doesn't this support the fact that most of us have a certain agenda we would like to see others adopt?

The truth is that we describe situations and events not as they are but as *we* are. Ideology is a prism through which we see reality and blame others for not seeing what we see. We should keep in mind what history has proven to be true: that what we see has no ultimate authority for all places and all times. A Chinese saying summarizes this point: "A person in a position of authority is a Confucian, because that doctrine supports the status quo. Out of power or office, they become Taoists, because Taoism rejects both worldly authority and individual responsibility. As death approaches, a person turns to Buddhism, because that faith offers hope of immortality."

> The seduction of idols is as short-lived as the moods that create them.

Another subtle aspect of living according to one's own authority is that we may not know when technology is misleading us. Advanced technology shows us what we can do and how far we can go, and that's great! But if we make idols of these human achievements, we will end up making ourselves—that is, human beings—the only reference point of truth, and we won't be able to transcend ourselves. In the long run, this could become stifling. For how long can we look at a skyscraper, a jet plane, a computer, a landing on the moon? These things are exciting for a while, and then we start to look for something else. The seduction of idols is as short-lived as the moods that create them. These attractions lack depth and enduring happiness.

There is something in us that wants to go farther, a certain sense of awe and reverence that seeks more than what is secondary or futile. We want to contemplate without end the starry skies, the soaring mountains, the green meadows, the beautiful lakes, and we do not feel bored when we do so. We want to go beyond ourselves and find God in the awesome might of a storm and say with the psalmist:

The voice of the Lord is over the waters;
> the God of glory thunders,
> the Lord, over mighty waters.

The voice of the Lord is powerful;
> the voice of the Lord is full of majesty.

The voice of the Lord
> causes the oaks to whirl,
> and strips the forest bare;
> and in his temple all say, "Glory!"

Ps 29:3, 9

The holy! There is something overwhelming, almost frightening, in encountering the holy, suggests Rudolph Otto in his book *The Idea of the Holy*. In the holy we learn that we are not the measure of the world but that there is a power much greater than our own power—no matter how powerful we are. To meet God is paradoxically more empowering, more comforting, and also more relaxing.

> There is something over-whelming, almost frightening, in encoun-tering the holy…

Being bound to an authority higher than my opinion or your opinion or the opinion of our idols gives us confidence and more assurance in our lives. There is something reassuring and permanently right about this authority. When we are in trouble, when we hesitate in making straightforward decisions, when we think it is so hard, so costly to go on with our commitments, we absolutely need to know that the path we are taking is the path that leads to God. We have to have faith. Faith heals our many limitations, problems, and infirmities on the individual level as well as on the social level. Faith shows us what must come first, and the first important thing is the first commandment.

The First Commandment

It is rare to meet individuals who really do not believe in God. But it is common to meet people—sometimes even among the members of clergy—who believe in dogmatic theology, the Bible, canon law, finance, administration for the common good of the Church, but who do not see God in the picture they present. The radical demand of the first commandment, "I am the Lord your God…you shall have no other gods before me" (Ex 20:2) can seem forgotten.

Offering sacrifice to stone statues or bowing down before golden calves are no longer common practices. Yet we have replaced these with other practices.

Our culture encourages us to look good at all costs, even if we have to lie to cover up our mistakes. We idolize our social gods such as prestige, possessions, pleasure, image, and personal knowledge. We may worship the god of naturalism, secular humanism, worldliness, inordinate affections, market-driven solutions, consumerism, empire-building theories, commercialization of religion, convenient pick-and-choose doctrines,

> Even though holiness requires effort, genuine sanctity is God's work.

and fanatic self-righteousness. We tend to confirm these popular phrases: "There are two ways of doing things: my way and the wrong way," and "My way or the highway." We absolutize our works—even good works such as teaching, giving to the poor, and saying prayers—while losing sight of God. In this way we waste our efforts and energies.

Jesus does not separate love of God and love of neighbor…

We should always keep in mind that there is no other God but the Lord. Even though holiness requires effort, genuine sanctity is God's work. Prayer, good works, even sanctity itself, are not supposed to be ends in themselves. Only God is our end and our source of holiness. Only this God can break through the illusions of our minds and hearts, and shatter any other gods we may worship.

The first commandment reminds us of God's actions in our lives: creating, sustaining, healing, guiding, and setting priorities. When we have this essential relationship with God, we will be compelled to enter into the other equally important relationship, that is, between ourselves and our neighbor. Jesus put it this way: "'You shall love the Lord your

God with all your heart, and with all your soul, and with all your mind.' This is the greatest and first commandment. And a second is like it: 'You shall love your neighbor as yourself'" (Mt 22:37-39).

Jesus does not separate love of God and love of neighbor; paganism does. Our God is transcendent and immanent, vertical and horizontal. Our God draws us to the divine center while pushing us toward others. The first commandment defines and readjusts our values and priorities by pointing us to the truth of God.

What Is Truth?

"What is truth?" (Jn 18:38), was Pilate's response when Jesus said, "Everyone who belongs to the truth listens to my voice" (Jn 18:37). Pilate walked away, not willing to hear an answer. We may blame Pilate for avoiding the truth, but like him, we too often walk away from the truth and from the experience of freedom Christ wants to give.

Jesus said, "If you continue in my word, you are truly my disciples; and you will know the truth, and the truth will make you free" (Jn 8:31–32). This "word" is the truth about God and the truth about ourselves. How painful it is, sometimes, to listen to this kind of truth! Because if we do, we ought to be willing to change, and this is usually not what we want to do. Isn't this why we run away, so that we do not have to hear the truth?

We are bound by invisible chains of lies. Multiple links from our culture, media, or even our family and friends force us, paradoxically in the name of freedom, to do things we don't want to do. We think that freedom is doing what we want to do, but in reality it is doing what we are meant to do. Are we free enough to do this?

> We think that freedom is doing what we want to do, but in reality it is doing what we are meant to do.

When we know and believe—really believe—that God loves us unconditionally and that we are meant to live in God's image, we realize that God's word is truth. "You will know the truth, and the truth will make you free" (Jn 8:32). Living a lie is inconsistent with the reality of a true God who is the truth. This is why we should "[Put] away falsehood" (Eph 4:25) and "Clothe [ourselves] with the new self, created according to the likeness of God in true righteousness and holiness"

(Eph 4:24). Truth is one of the pillars of faith.

Truth and healing go hand in hand. To be true is a loving thing to do for oneself and for others. A person of truth lives with sincerity, candor, and truthfulness in thought, word, and deed, casting away duplicity, dissimulation, and hypocrisy, which are fertile soil for many kinds of vices.

A lie contains the seeds of discord, deception, rejection, hurt, and resentment. It also tends to undermine trust in social relationships, greatly affect family life, and ruin careers and other aspects of our lives. Anxiety, stress, and depression are usually the consequences of such situations.

If truth is an interior renewal through faith in God, then truth will have the dynamism that enables us to overcome sin and its consequences and that guides us to full knowledge of the mystery of Christ and to the fulfillment of his law of love. It becomes a vital principle that directs the whole Christian life from within, "Because of the truth that abides in us and will be with us forever" (2 Jn 2).

"I am…the truth" (Jn 14:6), says the Lord. The closer we are to the Lord, the closer we are to the truth, and the better chance we have to be healed.

FOR YOUR REFLECTION & RESPONSE

1. Some of us have created idols that replace God. Do you have such images and idols? If yes, what are they? Where did they come from?

2. Does the world make sense to you? Who is in control in this world? Where can we find love, justice, and peace in a world full of violence, AIDS orphans, crippled children, and innocents who are being killed? Is becoming sick, growing old, and being depressed part of God's design for us? How does God let bad things happen? What—if anything—makes you doubt God's goodness and love? If God did not exist, what would be the scenario of our lives and of our world?

3. Why did you and I come into being? Is it realistic to trust God as the ultimate motivating force of the universe and especially of our world? Why do people need to believe in God? Is believing in God genetically and societally programmed? Do we really need God? If so, why is God not unmistakably known by all people?

4. Why do people feel, think, dream, live, and

die? What are your own dreams in the kingdom of God? What role does your faith play in the determination and realization of those dreams? Is God relevant in the design of your life? What best makes God real in your life? Do you really experience God in prayer?

5. Who is the God you believe in? Is faith just a good feeling for you? What would happen to your faith if there was no such feeling or if the feeling was gone, or if you felt that God was far away? Do you believe in the teachings of your spiritual tradition—all of it—or do you pick and choose? What would you do if your conscience was leading you one way and the rules of your community, your state, or the church were dictating another way?

6. Are you a religious person? Does belonging to a faith community and/or attending religious services help you increase your faith and bring you closer to God? Why? Do you have problems with organized religion? Do the Mass, the sacraments, and other prayers seem empty rituals or are they meaningful for you?

AFFIRMATION

Repeat this phrase several times a day:

I am God's child, and in the divine presence at all times.

PRAYER

Dear God, I desperately want to know the truth about you and about myself.

Teach me to think rightly about you and about myself. Remove the confusion and darkness that surrounds me. Reveal to me your light, your paths, your truth—my truth. Let me not find final answers anywhere except in you.

"Teach me, O Lord, the way of your statutes, and I will observe it to the end....Lead me in the path of your commandments, for I delight in it....I will never forget your precepts, for by them you have given me life" (Ps 119:33, 35, 93).

Please, God, set me free so that I can exist just for you. Amen.

CHAPTER TWO

The Inner Eye of Faith

"Faith is the assurance of things hoped for, the conviction of things not seen."

■ HEBREWS 11:1

Close your eyes for a moment. What do you see? You can see the page you were reading, the thought that was conveyed to you, and the transformed person you can become. You can see a faraway friend, a beautiful distant mountain, a full moon. You can see yourself on a trip to Europe, on a long journey toward a goal you wanted to reach, flying toward unlimited possibilities. You can also see Jesus feeding the multitude, teaching the Our Father to his disciples, hanging on the cross, being resurrected, and talking to you. Do you "see" God? That's faith.

God does not have to be in the flesh in order to be seen. The eye of your heart and mind, moved by God's grace, will lead you to see much more than you can see with the eyes of the body.

Faith Is More Than It Appears to Be

We often judge faith to be less than what it really is. In fact, it is more than it appears to be.

Faith is more than an emotion. Faith is not just a subjective feeling that God exists and that everything is all right because God is taking care of all things.

Faith is more than an opinion. In matters other than faith, we may have scientific evidence or a strong conviction based on rigorous rational analysis. But that is not the substance of faith. In faith, there is no evidence other than God's word. God's word is the evidence and the truth.

Faith is more than the truth that satisfies the intellect. Even though it does not destroy or deny what the intellect holds as true, faith may add more to what

> **Faith believes that change is not only possible but necessary.**

the intellect judges as objective truth. Thomas Keating, OCSO, co-founder of the Centering Prayer Movement, writes, "Faith is not just the assent of our minds to a series of dogmas….It is not a matter of understanding with our heads; it is the gift of our entire being to God—the ultimate reality. It orients us definitively in God's direction."

Faith is more than an act. Faith involves our entire attitude—indeed, our whole being—as well as the way we look at the world. It is seeing the mystery of the universe unfolding. It is seeing the plan of God through events, things, and people.

Faith is neither a presumption nor an assumption. As we have said before, faith is based on truth. When we presume or assume a truth we act without authority. When we deal with truth we cannot count on presumption and assumption. At the appearance of truth these simply vanish.

Faith is not fate. When we speak of fate it usually refers to approaching life with resignation and a sense of despair, that whatever will be will be. In fact, faith is the opposite of this attitude. Faith believes that change is not only possible but necessary. It makes change happen. William James said: "Believe that life is worth living and your belief will help create the fact." And George Bernard Shaw wrote: "You see things as they are; and you ask, 'Why?' But I dream things that never were; and I ask, 'Why not?'"

Faith is not knowing about God but knowing God. Knowledge is important, but it is not enough, and it is not always possible. The articles of faith are accepted as true even though they cannot always be understood and demonstrated as true beyond doubt. Thomas Aquinas, while insisting on the rationality of the Christian faith (remember his famous arguments for the existence of God?), insisted also on the fact that theology and faith are primarily a response to divine revelation. Indeed, we are called to know Jesus, not to know *about* him. Cardinal Newman once said: "We do not build cathedrals to intellectual principles but to persons. It is only by persons that we are subdued, melted, won over." Faith is not an object of knowledge as much as it is something to be lived. Jesus said: "I came that they may have life, and have it abundantly" (Jn 10:10).

> We are called to know Jesus, not to know *about* him.

Faith is more than a word found in the Bible or in a prayer. Although it is important to turn to the Bible and to prayer, a danger can emerge when we strive to find a verse or a prayer that witnesses to our spirit and need. Faith is not born out of an appropriate verse or a convenient prayer, but out of a truly intimate relationship with God.

Faith and religion are close partners, but they are not the same.

Faith is not faith in our faith but faith in God. The risk of having faith in our faith is the doubt we may put on its quality. Then, we begin to question the degree of its adequacy. This won't be the case if we have total faith in God: God's faithfulness, wisdom, power, goodness, and capacity to hear and answer our prayers.

Faith is more than just religion. Faith and religion are close partners, but they are not the same. Faith is like the soul of an experience, while religion is like the body of the experience. One is invisible; the other is external. One is a conviction; the other is an embodiment of this conviction. Faith is the deep relationship between a person and God; religion is the outer expression of this relationship.

It is risky not to make this distinction because confusing faith with religion can produce the opposite of faith, that is, atheism. This may breed prejudice, violence, oppression, and intolerance. This is the kind of atheistic faith that kills, not saves. We must disbelieve certain gods to find the true God. In this sense, Christ did not believe in false gods, and was crucified because he was accused of blasphemy and atheism. Christ did not want a sociological religion. He had more faith in the sinners, publicans, and pagans than in the priests, righteous, Pharisees, scribes, and theologians of the time.

Faith is more than hope. Faith is not a mere hope or expectation of future events but an acceptance, in a real way, of what has been promised.

Faith is more than just adherence to a catalogue of beliefs, tradition, and status quo. Bernard Häring, CSsR, a writer, scholar, pastor, and preacher, wrote in his book *Hope Is the Remedy*:

> When faith is approached by reason alone, it is presented as a system of well-defined truths, a catalogue of beliefs in an Establishment theology strongly influenced by canon law. Of course, there are abiding truths, it cannot be denied, but only in the One and through the One who is the

fullness of truth. Our human concepts are never the full truth; they are tainted by the pilgrim situation of the thinker....Tradition is a torrent of life; it is alive because of the presence of the living God in the ongoing history of salvation.

Faith does not suggest that we believe something but rather that we believe *in* someone. In this regard, certain beliefs can get in the way of and even impede true faith.

What Is Faith, Then?

In our Christian tradition we constantly talk about faith. But what is it that we are really talking about?

Paul defines faith this way: "Faith is the assurance of things hoped for, the conviction of things not seen" (Heb 11:1). Augustine asks: "What is faith save to believe what you do not see?" Thomas Aquinas affirms that "Faith is a habit of mind, which begins eternal life in us, and induces a reasonable assent to things unseen." Blaise Pascal explains: "Faith declares what the senses do not see, but not the contrary of what they see. It is above them, not the contrary of them."

Faith, therefore, means a free surrender to the unseen, untried, and unknown goodness of God. Faith unites the soul, mind, heart, and will with the eternal, invisible, and unthinkable word of God. But, as always, it is God who takes the initiative by giving faith to us as a gift. "Faith," wrote Thomas Merton, "is therefore a gratuitous gift of God....It is given to those who are disposed to accept the gift in simplicity and humility of heart, trusting not in the authority of political power or human prestige, but in the word of God speaking in the Church (see Mt 11:25–27)." Faith is a light infused by God directly into the soul without passing by the senses or even the intellect.

> **Faith means a free surrender to the unseen, untried, and unknown goodness of God.**

A primary cause sets all other causes in motion. This has been proven by Aristotle and other philosophers. Although this is true, it does not say enough about the God who is love—the living God. The God who is the living God is not a philosopher's abstraction, but the God of Abraham, Isaac, and Jacob. Our God is the Father of Jesus Christ and is revealed totally in him.

The "yes" of faith to this God indicates our readiness to be part of a community of believers who hear the universal call to holiness in action. In the words of the Second Vatican Council, "Every person should walk unhesitatingly according to his own personal gifts and duties in the path of a living faith, which arouses hopes and works through charity" (*Lumen Gentium*, 41).

In faith, we recognize that everything comes from God, and what we receive we want to share with others.

In faith, we recognize that everything comes from God...

In faith, our acceptance of the word of God is given to us by God in spite of the absence of logical proofs and scientific evidence. This is the hardest part of faith, indeed. The grace of God surpasses our anthropological and psychological understanding.

In faith, we declare our deep connection to the Church and its role in maintaining faith. The *Catechism of the Catholic Church* says: "'Believing' is an ecclesial act. The Church's faith precedes, engenders, supports, and nourishes our faith. The Church is the mother of all believers" (No. 181).

In faith, we declare our excitement at being loved

by God. We strive to share this love with others and bring others to share this same love with us.

In faith, we adhere to the whole of God's revelation, and we strive to bring this revelation to others.

In faith, we live the reality of the kingdom of God, and we strive to make the kingdom of God a reality in our world.

In faith, we live hope, justice, and love, and we strive to bring hope, justice, and love to places where they do not exist. Thus we will witness, as the Second Vatican Council says, "The birth of a new humanism, one in which man is defined first of all by his responsibility toward his brothers and toward history" (*Gaudium et Spes*, 55). Faith builds the earthly city, too.

In faith, God's grace permeates our whole being and our "entire life, including its worldly dimensions" (*Gaudium et Spes*, 21), making us more like Christ, allowing us to join God's love for all people, strengthening us to put into practice whatever heals any personal or societal crisis, and making us true members of the kingdom of God. Avery Dulles, SJ, wrote,

This means that through faith we become instruments in the healing and reconciliation of the broken world. We become agents of justice and bearers of the power of the kingdom. Faith, therefore, is more than intellectual assent, more than hope in what God will do without us; it is also a present participation in the work that God is doing—that is to say, in the task of bringing forth justice to nations.

In faith, we know God's plan for us and "cooperate with the divine will." In the words of the Second Vatican Council:

All of Christ's faithful, therefore, whatever be the conditions, duties, and circumstances of their lives, will grow in holiness day by day through these very situations, if they accept all of them with faith from the hand of their heavenly Father, and if they cooperate with the divine will by showing every man through their earthly activities the love with which God has loved the world (*Lumen Gentium*, 41).

Even though faith can be defined as an assent to the revealed doctrine and the acceptance of God's word, it is God's power within us that makes us whole and heals the infirmities of our personal and social existence. The American theologian Peter C. Hodgson wrote in his book *New Birth of Freedom*: "Faith is a *liberating power* that 'saves' life, giving it wholeness and efficacy, in the midst of bondage, estrangement and guilt." Faith is not a mental exercise. It comes from the living God to "[make] all things new" (Rev 21:5).

Faith helps see the unity and dignity of all people because we believe that everyone is made in the image and likeness of God (see Gen 1:26).

Faith is dynamic, not static. It is alive and must grow or it dies. It is an irrevocable commitment to Christ, who said with an irresistible magnetism, "I am the way, and the truth, and the life" (Jn 14:6), "And I, when I am lifted up from the earth, will draw all people to myself" (Jn 12:32).

Faith helps us find God in all that we do every day, make good use of all that God created, and bring the divine power to touch and heal every area of human suffering. Faith helps us trust God in every circumstance, even in troubled times. St. Teresa of Avila expresses this trust in this beautiful prayer:

Let nothing trouble you
Let nothing frighten you
Everything passes
God never changes
Patience obtains all
Whoever has God

Wants for nothing
God alone is enough.

Faith opens our minds to acknowledge realities that cannot be verified by science, such as hope, love, beauty, and heroism. It gives us a taste of eternal life. The *Catechism* states: "Faith makes us taste in advance the light of the beatific vision, the goal of our journey here below. Then we shall see God 'face to face' (1 Cor 13:12), 'as he is' (Jn 3:2). So faith is already the beginning of eternal life" (No. 163).

Faith is not for fanatics because they think they have all the answers. It is not for skeptics because for these there are no sufficient answers. It is not for the indifferent because they are interested neither in the questions nor in the answers. Faith is for the humble, the trusting, the earnest and passionate people for whom there is no room for wavering or mediocrity.

Faith is like the sap of a tree. We cannot see the sap, but without it there is no hope for the tree. "Faith," wrote William James, "is the habitual center of man's personal energies."

With faith, we can do impossible

> Faith opens our minds to acknowledge realities that cannot be verified by science...

things. We can even move mountains (see Mt 17:20–21), as the Son of God has authorized us to do. This means that anything we really believe can become reality. This is how God designed our human nature.

Examples of Faith

Abraham, who has been described as the Columbus of faith, is "the ancestor of all who believe" (Rom 4:11). When God said to him, "I have made you the ancestor of a multitude of nations" (Gen 17:5), there was no evidence to support God's statement. Abraham could not see the generations to come, but he believed God's promise in faith. He believed that God "calls into existence the things that do not exist" (Rom 4:17). He believed that what God promises, God will make happen.

Abraham's faith was characterized by obedience: "By faith Abraham obeyed when he was called to set out for a place that he was to receive as an inheritance" (Heb 11:8); by trust: "[Abraham] set out, not knowing where he was going" (Heb 11:8); by promise and expectation: "[Calling] into existence the things that do not exist" (Rom 4:17); and by surrendering to God's will when he was asked to sacrifice his son, Isaac. Faith seems to blossom when people are challenged by the difficulties of life and the winds of trial. Abraham proved this.

Abraham lived among a people that believed in many gods. There were gods of agriculture, storms, and fertility, to mention just a few. But the God of Abraham was responsible for all of creation, personally involved in the life and history of the people. This God asked Abraham to depart to a new land, leaving territory, house, property, family, and friends, along with cherished beliefs and practices. Abraham's liberation lay in the fact that, in faith, he could do nothing but count on God's promise.

Moses was a liberator, called by God to go to Pharaoh and seek the liberation of the enslaved Hebrew people. He was reluctant to do so, protesting, "Who am I that I should go to Pharaoh, and bring the Israelites out of Egypt?" (Ex 3:11). In other words, how could a simple man confront Egypt's might and liberate a people? But God assured of Moses, "I will be with you" (Ex 3:12). This meant that God would provide the necessary strength to successfully accomplish the mission.

Oppression has taken many forms down through the centuries: slavery, exploitation, brutal dictatorship, economic dependence, denial of religious freedom, degradation, prejudice, violence, terrorism, injustice, institutional poverty, and other oppressive and unhealthy conditions. All these and more can be our "pharaohs." God knows it. We may be like Moses and say, "Who am I that I should go to pharaoh?" Then, an answer comes from heaven and from the depth of our soul and heart: "I will be with you."

Moses had faith. Paul wrote: "By faith he [Moses] left Egypt, unafraid of the king's anger; for he persevered as though he saw him who is invisible" (Heb 11:27). By faith, we, too, can leave behind all the unhealthy conditions of our own pharaoh, whatever it may be, and count on the one who will be with us and support us in our confrontations.

> By faith, we, too, can leave behind all the unhealthy conditions of our own pharaoh, whatever it may be…

David was chosen by God to be the king of Israel. In this capacity, he made Jerusalem the center of Hebrew culture and worship. But David was not without serious fault. He committed adultery, then sent the woman's husband out to be killed in battle. Can a person sink lower that that? In spite of all this, God said, "I have found David, son of Jesse, to be a man after my heart, who will carry out all my wishes" (Acts 13:22).

The motive behind such preference by God may have been David's faith. His inexcusable errors were not deliberate acts of disobedience to God's will, but passionate outbursts of an impulsive nature. Indeed, his incomparable psalms eloquently describe his spiritual struggle to develop a deeper holiness and an attitude of greater surrender toward God.

Psalm 51 remains one of the most amazing descriptions of religious experience of all time. On the one hand, it speaks of the darkest side of sin; on the other hand, it is a clear act of faith and trust in God's mercy. It recognizes the power of grace to forgive and even eradicate every trace of guilt and corruption, and to restore the sinner to God's original blessing. In one breath, David admitted, "My sin is ever before me....I was born guilty....Blot out all my iniquities" (Ps 51:3, 5, 9); while in another breath, he confidently confirmed, "I shall be clean....I shall be whiter than snow....I will teach transgressors your ways, and sinners will return to you" (Ps 51:7, 13). Identifying the sin that was committed, without palliation or excuse, is significant to David's faith. Equally significant is lifting up the soul to a place of justification and salvation:

Commit your way to the Lord;
trust in him, and he will act.
He will make your vindication
shine like the light,
and the justice of your cause
like the noonday. (Ps 37:5–6)

David's faith was an alchemy that turned his sins, sorrow, and shame into lessons for others. After his reconciliation, his life's purpose was to lead sinners to God and to turn every situation in life to a way of blessing for others.

The fact that God produced amazing results from Abraham's blindness, Moses' inadequacy, and David's broken life is an incentive to keep us from discouragement, despair, and depression. To have—like Abraham, Moses, and David—a soul, mind, heart, eyes, and purpose directed toward God can guarantee the optimum conditions for our own healing.

FOR YOUR REFLECTION & RESPONSE

1. Do you know someone who has a strong faith? Do you see any difference between this person's behavior and the behavior of others? Is faith more important than good conduct? What dif-

ference does it make in your own life if you have or don't have faith? Do you believe that your faith makes a difference in the world as a whole? How can you live by faith in a confusing world?

2. Sigmund Freud thought that faith was an invention of the subconscious. What makes you believe that Jesus is the Lord? How can you be sure? How would you defend your faith to a non-believer?

3. Almost every great person of faith, from Abraham to Mother Teresa of Calcutta, carried others with them in their mission. What is the secret of their driving force? Do you have such a driving force, or know of someone who does?

4. Christian faith recommends practice of the virtue of patience. Is patience a proof that one has faith? What difference do you see between secular optimism and happiness, and Christian faith and joy? Have you ever experienced a situation that required uncompromising faith from you? What promise does faith hold for you?

5. Abraham, Moses, David and other faith-heroes were not perfect people. What connec-

tion do you see between faith, character, and conduct? You may have someone in your life whose conversation and conduct tend to be faith-destroying. How do you deal with this person? Do scandals in your own community or in the church at large affect your faith? Why?

AFFIRMATION

Repeat this phrase several times a day:

I see God at work in my life.

PRAYER

Dear God, may I have the faith of your prophets, saints, and martyrs. May I not worry about my past, my present, or my future. You are in charge. May I surrender to your will. Your plan for me is certainly right. May you be at the forefront of my life.

I will follow in your footsteps. In you I trust. "To whom can [I] go?" (Jn 6:68) In you I have faith. Nothing else really matters. May I never forget that you and I together can handle any challenge. Amen.

CHAPTER THREE

Faith Therapy

"Truly I tell you, if you have faith the size of a mustard seed, you will say to the mountain, 'Move from here to there,' and it will move; and nothing will be impossible for you."

■ MATTHEW 17:20‑21

"Take heart, it is I; do not be afraid," said Jesus to his disciples whose boat was "battered by the waves…for the wind was against them" (Mt 14:24–27). Then Jesus allowed Peter to walk on the water toward him.

Everything was all right until Peter realized how strong the wind was. He became afraid. He doubted. He lost sight of Jesus and started to sink. "He cried out, 'Lord, save me!' Jesus immediately reached out his hand and caught him, saying, 'You of little faith, why did you doubt?'" (Mt 14:30–31).

Like Peter, we may have the winds of life against us: failures, illness, broken hearts, losses, and many other aggravations. We may have the waves crashing hard against all sides of our boat. We may become per-plexed, confused, rejected, and close to despair. What do we do? Peter's solution was to say, "Lord, if it is you, command me to come to you on the water" (Mt 14:28). And Peter started to walk across the water.

God does impossible things.

God wants us to do impossible things as well. Jesus said: "Truly I tell you, if you have faith the size of a mustard seed, you will say to the mountain, 'Move from here to there,' and it will move; and nothing will be impossible for you" (Mt 17:20–21).

How Mountains Can Be Moved

The mountains in our lives may seem immovable. We might be bending under too much stress and too many adversities. We might be suffering from many weaknesses and incurable diseases. But when we place

Faith gives us the power to rise above any challenge.

our faith in God, sincerely and truly, we set into motion a powerful force that has the ability to change situations and create new realities. We know that God will help us move the mountains that crush us. This is what Jesus promised if we "have faith the size of a mustard seed." With God, nothing is impossible (see Mk 10:27).

Faith gives us the power to rise above any challenge. It helps us adjust and heal in any situation. For like the bird that starts to sing in the darkness of the early morning, knowing that a new day is coming soon, we will realize that, even in our darkest night a new day will give birth to second chances and new possibilities. We are free to reach the stars.

Perhaps Jesus' greatest gift was to convince us that we are children of God with divine, unlimited potential. He said, "Very truly, I tell you, the one who believes in me will also do the works that I do and, in fact, will do greater works than these, because I am going to the Father. I will do whatever you ask in my name, so that the Father may be glorified in the Son. If in my name you ask me for anything, I will do it" (Jn 14:12–14). By this understanding, our lives are bound to be changed forever.

Even though faith deals with impossibilities, it should not replace physical prowess, human research, and traditional medicine. Faith should not be subject to any obstacle or any so-called impossibility.

It is important to think, look, and act in a way that shows God is fully alive. As we flood our minds, hearts, and wills with expressions of faith, our faith will grow and continue to grow, affecting all that we hope for in our lives. We are connected to God's power.

Faith, a gift and a fruit of the Spirit, is what roots are to a mighty oak tree. When fierce winds blow, the oak tree stands firm and secure because it has deep and strong roots. Our beliefs are our roots. The adversities of life won't break us down when our faith is strong. Paradoxically, adversity has the potential to make us even stronger.

Faith's Healing Factor

To be truly alive requires faith. If you keep saying sincerely, "Lord, I believe" (Mk 9:24), soon, with God's grace, what you ask for will become real. Notice that the father in Mark 9:24 didn't just say, "I believe." He said, "Lord, I believe," to indicate there is more in the healing process than what human psychology and

> The adversities of life won't break us down when our faith is strong.

psychiatry can offer. We need the help of our all-powerful God so we can say with Paul, "I can do all things through him who strengthens me" (Phil 4:13).

A strong faith shapes reality. We don't see things as they are; we see things as we believe they are. Strong faith re-creates the world. This is why we can say that the content of our belief is more important than reality. And this is why faith has a great influence on health and healing.

Cardiologist Herbert Benson, a pioneer in mind/body medicine who wrote *The Relaxation Response*, says, "Just having a strong belief is enough to cause things to happen in our physiology, but this is a very ticklish point. It does seem that just the state of belief, which can emanate from a variety of personal, philosophical, or religious orientations, is itself a powerful force." The power of this faith is so great that, as Benson believes, it can help relieve headaches and control angina pain, hypertension, insomnia, back aches, panic attacks, and other diseases related to stress and anxiety.

Also, Dale A. Matthews, an internist on the faculty of Georgetown University School of Medicine, suggests that faith in God seems to have influence not only on the healing of physical and emotional problems, but also on an improved quality of life. Matthews wrote: "When studied scientifically, religious commitment has been generally found to have significant health benefits. In a review of more than 200 published studies of the linkage between religion and health status, seventy-five percent revealed a positive relationship."

While exploring the relationship between juveniles' faith and committing crimes, more recent studies found that families with a strong faith life are less likely to be dysfunctional or to produce children who commit crimes. Commenting on these studies, Willard M. Oliver, assistant professor of criminal justice at Radford University in Virginia, wrote, "When a youth identifies himself as Catholic and believes strongly in his faith, coupled with his holy obligation to attend Mass every Sunday and when involved in a church group, the chances of him committing juvenile crimes or exhibiting delinquent behavior fall dramatically. The key to the prevention of youth crime for Catholic families should be very evident: family and strong Catholic faith."

Jeff Levin, a social epidemiologist and writer, asks these questions in his book, *God, Faith, and Health*:

What does faith do for a person? Does faith instill a certain mind-set? A perspective about one's life or place in the world? Are people with more faith better equipped in some way to meet challenges without succumbing to stress? To resist the disease-inducing effects of certain exposures or risk factors? Are there particular thought patterns or mental processes associated with faith that are beneficial for health and well-being?

I believe all these questions can be answered affirmatively. I propose that faith benefits physical and mental health specifically by promoting hope, optimism, and positive expectations. These cognitions are, by definition, functions of faith. They in turn influence our health and well-being.

Harold G. Koenig, director of the Center for the Study of Religion, Spirituality, and Health at Duke University Medical Center, observes:

In fact, religious coping was the only...factor that significantly predicted better mental health outcomes....These are not isolated findings. Numerous investigators, working in different areas of the country, have reported similar findings. These studies suggest that older persons who use religion in this manner experience lower rates of depression, have higher self-esteem, and appear to live longer.

How does faith affect health in general and why it is so powerful?

When we have deep faith, we activate the mind's energy, which is part of our universal energy. This causes circumstances and events to be created so that we can achieve our goals. If we become restless and dissatisfied with our status quo, this could be a sign that faith is trying to implement ideas of greater good in our lives. Author Charles Fillmore compares this phenomenon to an electric current when he writes:

> Just as the electric current precipitates certain metals in an acid solution, so faith stirs into action the electrons of man's brain; and concurrently with the spiritual ethers, these electrons hasten nature and produce quickly what ordinarily would require months of seed-time and harvest.

> When we have deep faith, we activate the mind's energy, which is part of our universal energy.

Faith is a potent fountain of spiritual, emotional, and physical energy. We should watch carefully whatever we turn our attention to, whatever convictions we hold, and whatever expectations we harbor. When we have faith (see Lk 17:19), we can be transformed by the renewal of our minds (see Rom 12:2), to which Paul gave this prescription (Phil 4:4-7):

Rejoice in the Lord always; again I will say, Rejoice. Let your gentleness be known to everyone. The Lord is near. Do not worry about anything, but in everything by prayer and supplication with thanksgiving let your requests be made known to God. And the peace of God, which surpasses all understanding, will guard your hearts and your minds in Christ Jesus.

Koenig concluded from his research that faith helps patients in five ways.

• First, faith gives them hope for healing as well as hope for life after death.
• Second, faith gives them a sense of control by trusting in God who will answer their prayers.
• Third, in faith they can face illness with strength.
• Fourth, in faith they find meaning to their life, illness, and pain.
• Fifth, in faith they find a sense of purpose.

Hope, control, strength, meaning, and purpose make us feel better. We are happier, more satisfied with our lives and relationships, and we have more self-respect and higher self-esteem. Such positive feelings and thoughts, as studies and common sense show, should trigger brain activity that produces the favorable conditions necessary for healing. But it is imperative to possess a real desire to let go of illness. If we unconsciously have a need to hold on to our illness for one reason or another—the need for attention from others, for example—our chances of healing diminish considerably.

This process of healing is not only and simply a kind of placebo effect that suggests, as oncologist and surgeon Bernie Siegel writes, "that we may be able to change what takes place in our bodies by changing our state of mind." It is a humble recognition that we cannot do it alone, and that we need divine intervention to help us get out of the trouble we are in. "We act in faith," said the late diplomat Däg Hammerskjöld, "and miracles occur." We may not know how they occur, but they occur. They are there. Every minute of our life is a miracle—a grace from God, indeed.

Zoroaster, a Persian philosopher from the sixth century BC, had the following wisdom about healing:

One may heal with holiness.
One may heal with the law.
One may heal with knife.
One may heal with herbs.
One may heal with the Holy Word: This one it is, that will best drive away sickness from the body of the faithful.

For this is the best healing of all remedies.

The Holy Word

The Holy Word, for us, is Jesus Christ. Through his life, the miracles he performed, and especially in his teachings, Jesus placed special emphasis on the persistence of faith. The gospels report, "When he entered the house, the blind men came to him; and Jesus said to them, 'Do you believe that I am able to do this?' They said to him, 'Yes, Lord.' Then he touched their eyes and said, 'According to your faith let it be done to you.' And their eyes were opened" (Mt 9:28–30).

"You of little faith, why did you doubt?" (Mt 14:31).

"The disciples came to Jesus privately and said, 'Why could we not cast [the demon] out?' He said to them, 'Because of your little faith.' If you have faith the size of a mustard seed, you will say to this mountain, 'Move from here to there,' and it will move; and nothing will be impossible for you" (Mt 17:19-21).

"All things can be done for the one who believes" (Mk 9:23).

"And these signs will accompany those who believe: by using my name they will cast out demons; they will speak in new tongues; they will pick up snakes in their hands, and if they drink any deadly thing, it will not hurt them; they will lay their hands on the sick, and they will recover" (Mk 16:17–18).

"Do not doubt but believe" (Jn 20:27).

"This is the work of God, that you believe in him whom he has sent" (Jn 6:29).

An interesting story about the power of faith is found in the Gospel of Matthew (15:21–28). Upon encountering Jesus, a Canaanite woman shouted, "Have mercy on me, Lord, Son of David; my daughter is tormented by a demon." Jesus said, "I was sent only to the lost sheep of the house of Israel." Discrimination, right? Wrong. "Lord, help me," she persisted. Jesus answered, "It is not fair to take the children's food and throw it to the dogs." Arrogance, right? Wrong again. The woman said, "Yes, Lord, yet even the dogs eat the crumbs that fall from

> Every minute of our life is a miracle…

their masters' table." At that moment, Jesus answered her, "Woman, great is your faith! Let it be done for you as you wish." And her daughter was healed.

What is going on here? One plausible explanation is this: at that time, the Canaanites were despised by the Jews, who called them dogs, because they worshiped statues of a goddess. This is a historical and cultural fact. When Jesus reminded the woman of her cultural condition, he wanted to heal her as well as her daughter from the hurt of being called "dog." He wanted to cast off all bitterness from the environment where healing was going to take place. That's healing. One does not heal without getting rid of old hurts, resentments, and bitterness.

God will heal our wounds, meet our needs, and transform our lives spiritually, emotionally, and physically.

Another striking story occurs when Jesus met the Samaritan woman at the well (Jn 4:7–42). After a very personal conversation with Christ, the woman went back to her village to report, "Come and see a man who told me everything I have ever done!" (Jn 4:29). This woman, whose several broken relationships indicated deep and untold wounds, felt no judgment from a man of compassion and understanding such as Jesus. She felt freed by an embodied, forgiving love to say what she had kept hidden from others, and even from herself. Her feelings about herself, others, and God had changed.

Emotional healing is part of spiritual healing. If we allow God to show us all that we have done, God will heal our wounds, meet our needs, and transform our lives spiritually, emotionally, and physically. We become whole again. This is what the sacrament of reconciliation does. It helps us become whole and live a new life of grace.

The image we have of Jesus would not be complete if we consider him a mere teacher and preacher of religious truth. The many miracles, from exorcism to his extraordinary power over the forces of nature, attest to his healing activity. Matthew reported that "Jesus went throughout Galilee, teaching in their synagogues and proclaiming the good news of the kingdom and curing every disease and every sickness among the people. So his fame spread throughout all Syria, and they brought to him all the sick, those who were afflicted with various diseases and pains, demoniacs, epileptics, and paralytics, and he cured them" (Mt 4:23–24).

Jesus also gave this power of healing to his apostles: "Jesus called the twelve together and gave them power and authority over all demons and to cure diseases, and he sent them out to proclaim the kingdom of God and to heal" (Lk 9:1–2). They did this, as reported in the Acts of the Apostles: "Peter said, 'I have no silver or gold, but what I have I give you; in the name of Jesus Christ of Nazareth, stand up and walk.' And he took him by the right hand and raised him up; and immediately his feet and ankles were made strong. Jumping up, he stood and began to walk, and he entered the temple with them, walking and leaping and praising God" (Acts 3:6–8).

Paul and the other disciples did similar work (Acts 5:12–16; 2:42–47). And this is what healers throughout the ages still do when they perform healing services in the name of Jesus Christ.

When you have a problem, bring Jesus into it; you will notice the difference this makes. Do it because you are God's child (Jn 1:12), Christ's friend (Jn 15:15), a member of Christ's body (1 Cor 12:27), and complete in Christ (Col 2:10).

And when you are united with the Lord and are one spirit with him (1 Cor 6:17), every power belongs to you.

Healing from Scripture

Every power belongs to those who believe

When you feel…	Remember
Weary	"The way of the Lord is a strong–hold for the upright" (Prov 10:29).
Paralyzed by fear	"God did not give us a spirit of cowardice, but rather a spirit of power and of love and of self-discipline" (2 Tim 1:7).
Defeated	"[God] gives us the victory through our Lord Jesus Christ" (1 Cor 15:57).
Helpless	"I can do all things through him who strengthens me" (Phil 4:13).
Sick	"Your faith has made you well; go in peace, and be healed of your disease" (Mk 5:34).
Worthless	"God created humankind in his image" (Gen 1:27).
Weak and useless	"He [the Lord] said to me, 'My grace is sufficient for you, for

power is made perfect in weakness.' So, I will boast all the more gladly of my weaknesses, so that the power of Christ may dwell in me" (2 Cor 12:9).

Needing approval "Am I now seeking human approval, or God's approval? Or am I trying to please people? If I were still pleasing people, I would not be servant of Christ." (Gal 1:10); "Whatever your task, put yourselves into it, as done for the Lord and not for your masters, since you know that from the Lord you will receive the inheritance as your reward" (Col 3:23-24).

FOR YOUR REFLECTION & RESPONSE

1. Have you observed circumstances in your life that caused illness through negative feelings and thoughts of despair? Have you experienced, or known someone who experienced, a recovery because of faith? Do you consider faith and hope an integral part of "the whole armor of God"

(Eph 6:11) that can protect someone from harm- ful conditions? Can you imagine a life without faith? What does it look like? Do you worry too much about the future at the expense of the present, as if God doesn't care about your future?

2. Faith can heal our scars, the emotional hurts and guilt feelings from the past. Bring the light of faith to some of these experiences in your life and put them in a different perspective. Does faith help you interpret them in a new light? Because of your faith, do you feel more hopeful, more optimistic, and more confident? Does faith give you a reason for living and a sense of purpose? Do you expect God to answer your prayers?

3. God's will is that we live happy, healthy, and holy lives and enjoy all God's favors. So why don't more people live this way? Does God's will moti- vate your life? Is the God you believe in the one who loves us and has promised never to forsake us? Do you turn to God in your need as well as when everything is going well? Do you dare to be vulnerable to and live in deep intimacy with God?

4. Why do some people stay well and happy, or get well when they are sick, while others live

most of their lives in misery? Is this fair? Does our understanding of justice and fairness fit with God's justice and fairness?

5. Do you wonder sometimes if Jesus is real and available to you the way he was available to his disciples? What do you think might happen—a sense of purpose, a meaning for what you do, and peace of mind and heart, for example—if you invite him into your life? Will he really refresh you when you are troubled, burdened, and stuck? Is his yoke really easy? Do you really believe that Jesus is the answer to all your needs, and that he will heal you if you ask him to do so?

AFFIRMATION

Repeat this phrase several times a day:

By the grace of God I am healthy, happy, and holy.

PRAYER

Lord, as you commanded Peter to cross the water (see Mt 14:24–27), command me now to come to you across the irritations, guilt feelings, troubles, and storms of my life.

Grant me the faith that enables me to face resolutely and firmly the many challenges in my life. May I never be tempted to forget the power of your love and care and redemption. May I recover from any negative attitudes, infirmities, or lack passion for life.

O divine physician, heal me, purify me, use me, and make me whole. Then let me bring your healing power to others so that they too may come to know your overwhelming mercy and love.

My dear Lord, grant me the chance to begin again, your way this time, with a new me made the way you want me to be—holy, happy, and healthy.

God, grant me the faith that works miracles. Amen.

Especially in times of crises, we need to know that the Spirit is closer to us than our very breath.

We are never powerless, left to struggle on our own. God is always there. Sometimes we forget this, but we must always have faith. We need to remember who we truly are.

The very core of our journey is to find the truth about God and about ourselves. How we see God tells us about ourselves, and makes all the difference in the world. The God of love, not the God of fear, helps us heal. There is a theological implication in the very act of healing.

Faith is full of wonder and full of power. It moves mountains and solves crises. It prevents breakdowns and heals illnesses. It revolutionizes thinking, changes hearts, and transforms lifestyles. It makes God alive here and now. This is the key to living a life blessed with wonders.

In faith we find our true identity as children of God. We recognize with gratitude that everything comes from the Father and that we can do all things by the power of Christ. We also discover the flame of the Holy Spirit that will allow us to radiate the Good News to the ends of the earth. This way, we help ourselves and everyone else overcome the spiritual crisis of the world, which is graver than its physical crisis.

In this mission, there is no room for mediocrity and false compromises. People of faith are on fire. They are passionate saints who are not concerned with the small satisfactions of life. They are committed to work not only for their own salvation but for the salvation of all. They deeply desire the coming of God's kingdom. They want God's will to be done on earth as it is in heaven.

The Bible confirms that, by faith, all things can be achieved. The secret, then, to getting what you want, healing included, is to approach it with faith. With a clear and daily act of faith, you send spiritual vitality through your personality, and you obtain the healing and the favor you are requesting. Faith is not a philosophical speculation about truth. Faith is a reason for living, loving, and sharing. Faith is a reason for dying. What is worth living for is worth dying for.

With faith, your worries diminish considerably. You feel secure because you no longer depend on yourself, but on God who does impossible things (see Mt 17:21; Phil 4:13). Faith gives great joy because it assures a new orientation, growth, and social concern for your life.

Because it is not merely a private matter, our faith should benefit the world. It should provide hope, strength, and healing to everyone we meet. And it does so without anxiety. "Have courage for the great sorrows of life and patience for the small ones," wrote Victor Hugo, "and when you have laboriously accomplished your daily task, go to sleep in peace. God is awake."

In faith, we have a vision—"A new heaven and a new earth" (Rev 21:1)—one to be shared with the entire world, "making all things new" (Rev 21:5). If the present seems bleak, the future must be brilliant. This is precisely what Jesus came to give us: a new life characterized by a loving relationship with himself and his Father through the Holy Spirit. Healing is the result of believing in the wonderful message of the Good News: Jesus saves us from sin as well as from emotional and physical sickness. Our faith is our healing gift for each other and for the world.

When we believe, we see God at work and we become participants in God's life and work.

With faith we leave our old country, as Abraham did, and we travel as Moses did toward the Promised Land—the kingdom of God. As Brother Laurence wrote, "All things are possible to him who believes."